Jobs Around Town

Shelly Buchanan, M.S.Ed.

Consultants

Shelley Scudder
Gifted Education Teacher
Broward County Schools

Caryn Williams, M.S.Ed.
Madison County Schools
Huntsville, AL

Publishing Credits

Dona Herweck Rice, *Editor-in-Chief*
Lee Aucoin, *Creative Director*
Torrey Maloof, *Editor*
Diana Kenney, M.A.Ed., NBCT, *Associate Education Editor*
Marissa Rodriguez, *Designer*
Stephanie Reid, *Photo Editor*
Rachelle Cracchiolo, M.S.Ed., Publisher

Image Credits: pp. 5, 11, 13, 18–19, 20 Alamy; p. 21 Anika Pachal; pp. 6, 9 Getty Images; p. 16 Time & Life Pictures/Getty Image; pp. 15, 17 iStockphoto; p. 8 The Library of Congress [LC-DIG-fsac-1a34131]; p. 10 The Library of Congress [LC-DIG-hec-09910]; p. 14 The Library of Congress [LC-DIG-ppmsca-06733]; p. 12 The Library of Congress [LC-USZ62-112973]; p. 24 The Library of Congress [LC-USZ62-112973]; p. 4 The Library of Congress [LC-USZ62-47295]; All other images from Shutterstock.

Teacher Created Materials
5301 Oceanus Drive
Huntington Beach, CA 92649-1030
http://www.tcmpub.com

ISBN 978-1-4333-6980-3

Printed by: 51497
Printed in: China

Table of Contents

Communities

Communities (kuh-MYOO-ni-teez) are places. People live there. People work there. People help make a community a special place.

This is a community in Virginia in 1915.

This is a community in Massachusetts today.

Goods and Services

Communities need people who do different jobs. Some people make and sell **goods**, or things. Some people sell **services**, or work.

This woman is shopping for goods in 1930.

Jobs Pay Off

People earn money for the work they do. Money helps them pay **bills** and buy food to eat.

This man is fixing a car today.

Bakers make yummy treats. Farmers grow food. They **support**, or help, their communities with the goods they sell.

A farmer plows a field in 1944.

A farmer sells food today.

Bankers help people save money. Mail carriers bring mail. They support their communities with the services they **provide**.

A mail carrier brings mail in 1917.

Rain and Snow!

Mail carriers in the United States bring mail in any weather. They work in the rain and snow.

A mail carrier brings mail today.

Care and Help

Doctors and nurses keep people well. Dentists take care of teeth. Communities need their services.

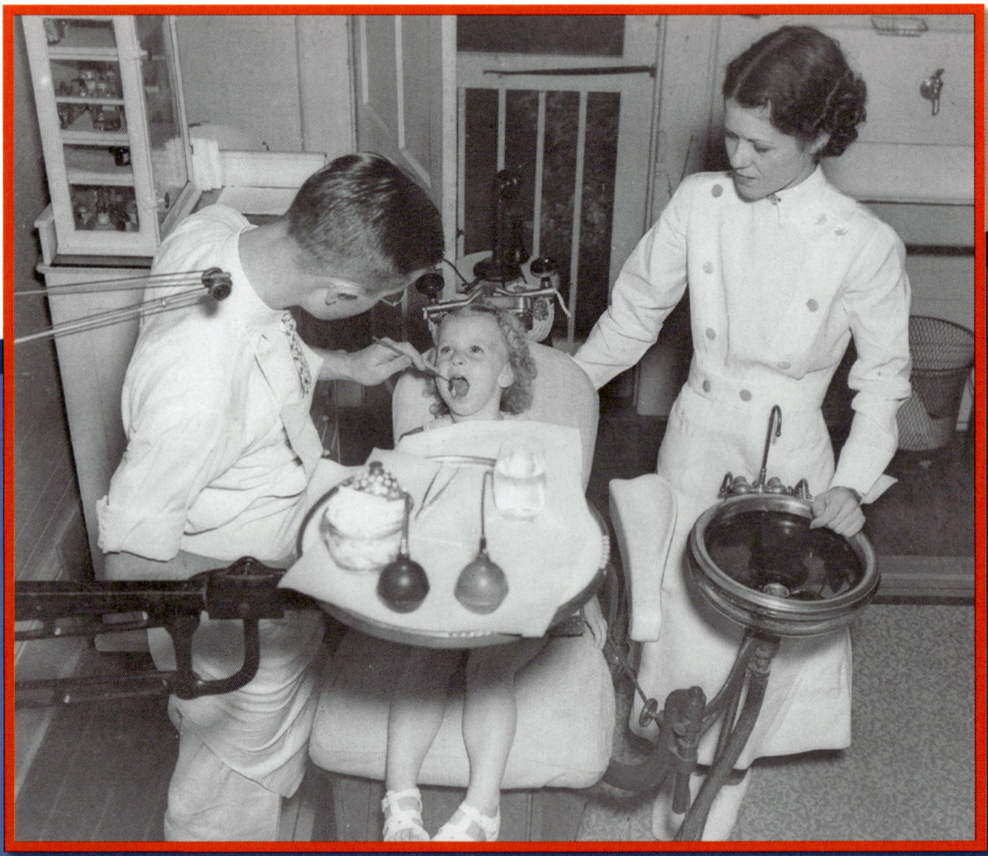

A dentist looks at a girl's teeth in 1942.

Special Doctors

There are many kinds of doctors. There are even special doctors for babies and kids!

A nurse checks on a boy today.

Firefighters put out fires. Teachers help kids learn. Communities need their services, too!

A student learns from his teacher in 1965.

Firefighters get ready to put out a fire today.

Many Kinds

There are many jobs in a community. There are many goods and services that are needed.

A trash collector picks up trash in 1942.

Keeping It Clean

Trash collectors keep our communities clean. They collect, **sort**, and take away our trash.

A trash collector picks up trash today.

Do Your Part

What job will you have some day? What good will you sell? What service will you provide?

POLICE

Learn It!

Ask an adult to help you learn about workers in your community. Talk with a worker. Learn about his or her job. Does he or she provide a good or a service?

This girl learns about being a firefighter.

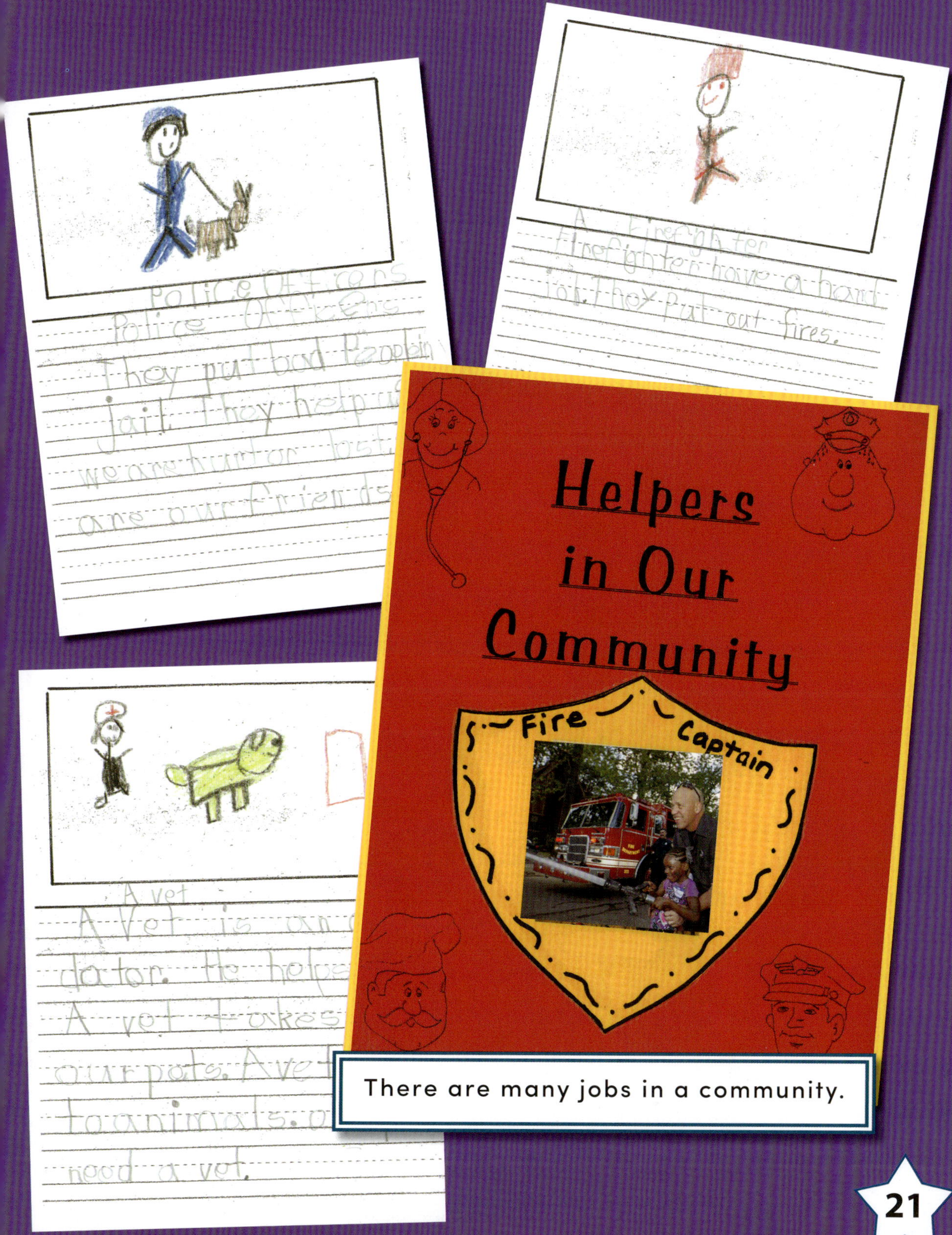

There are many jobs in a community.

Glossary

bills—papers that say how much money you owe

communities—places where groups of people live and work together

goods—things people can buy

provide—to give things that are wanted or needed

services—work or help for sale

sort—put in groups

support—to take care of

Index

Your Turn!

Then and Now

Kids went to the dentist long ago. Kids go to the dentist today, too! This photo shows a girl at the dentist long ago. How is your dentist the same? How is your dentist different?